THIS
IS
FOR
YOU
D0234699

SCEPTRE

WHEN I WAS SMALLER
WHEN I WAS A CHILD, A BOY
ONE MINUTE WORRYING, THE NEXT NOT HAVING A CARE.
I WOKE UP AND GOT DRESSED AND DID ALL THE THINGS THAT YOU DO ALL DAY

ALL THE FEELINGS YOU FEEL ALL DAY LONG.
FEELING SCARED AND THEN FEELING BRAVE AND THEN FEELING SCARED AGAIN
ALL DAY LONG EVERY THOUGHT AND BLINK AND FEAR
YOU ONLY DARE TO SHARE WITH YOURSELF

AND THEN FOR THE FIRST TIME
I BEGAN TO FEEL VERY ALONE

I WALKED
AND I THOUGHT
AND I WALKED
AND I THOUGHT
AND I THOUGHT
AND I WALKED
AND I THOUGHT
AND I WALKED
AND I THOUGHT
AND I WALKED
AND I THOUGHT

AND I WALKED
AND I THOUGHT
AND I WALKED
AND I THOUGHT
AND I THOUGHT
AND I WALKED
AND I WALKED
AND I THOUGHT

AND
STILL
THIS
FEELING
OF
BEING
ALONE
STAYED
AND
LINGERED
INSIDE
ME

IT'S NOT THAT I FEEL ALONE
BECAUSE I HAVE NO FRIENDS.
I HAVE LOTS OF FRIENDS.
I KNOW THAT I HAVE PEOPLE WHO CAN
HOLD ME
AND
REASSURE ME
AND
TALK TO ME
AND
CARE FOR ME
AND
THINK OF ME
BUT THEY CAN'T BE INSIDE MY HEAD
WITH ME ALL THE TIME –
FOR ALL TIME.

I MEAN, WELL WHAT I REALLY MEAN
I CAN'T EASILY EXPLAIN. EXCEPT THAT IN HERE -
IN THIS THING CALLED ME. THAT'S THE VERY
PROBLEM - IT IS ALWAYS JUST ME.
MYSELF ALONE. AND IT JUST ISN'T ENOUGH.

I TRIED TO ASK
OTHER PEOPLE IF THEY
FELT THIS WAY AS
WELL AND THEY
ALL SAID NO,
NEVER, NOT AT
ALL.... UNTIL
I FELT AS IF I
WAS GOING MAD.

I CRIED
AND I
SCREAMED
AT THE SKY
I DONT
WANT
TO FEEL
LIKE THIS
FOR THE REST OF
MY LIFE
BUT THE CLOUDS WERE INDIFFERENT TO MY TEARS
AND WHY SHOULD THEY CARE. THEY FLOAT AND
DRIFT AND JOIN TOGETHER AND PART AND REFORM FOR ETERNITY

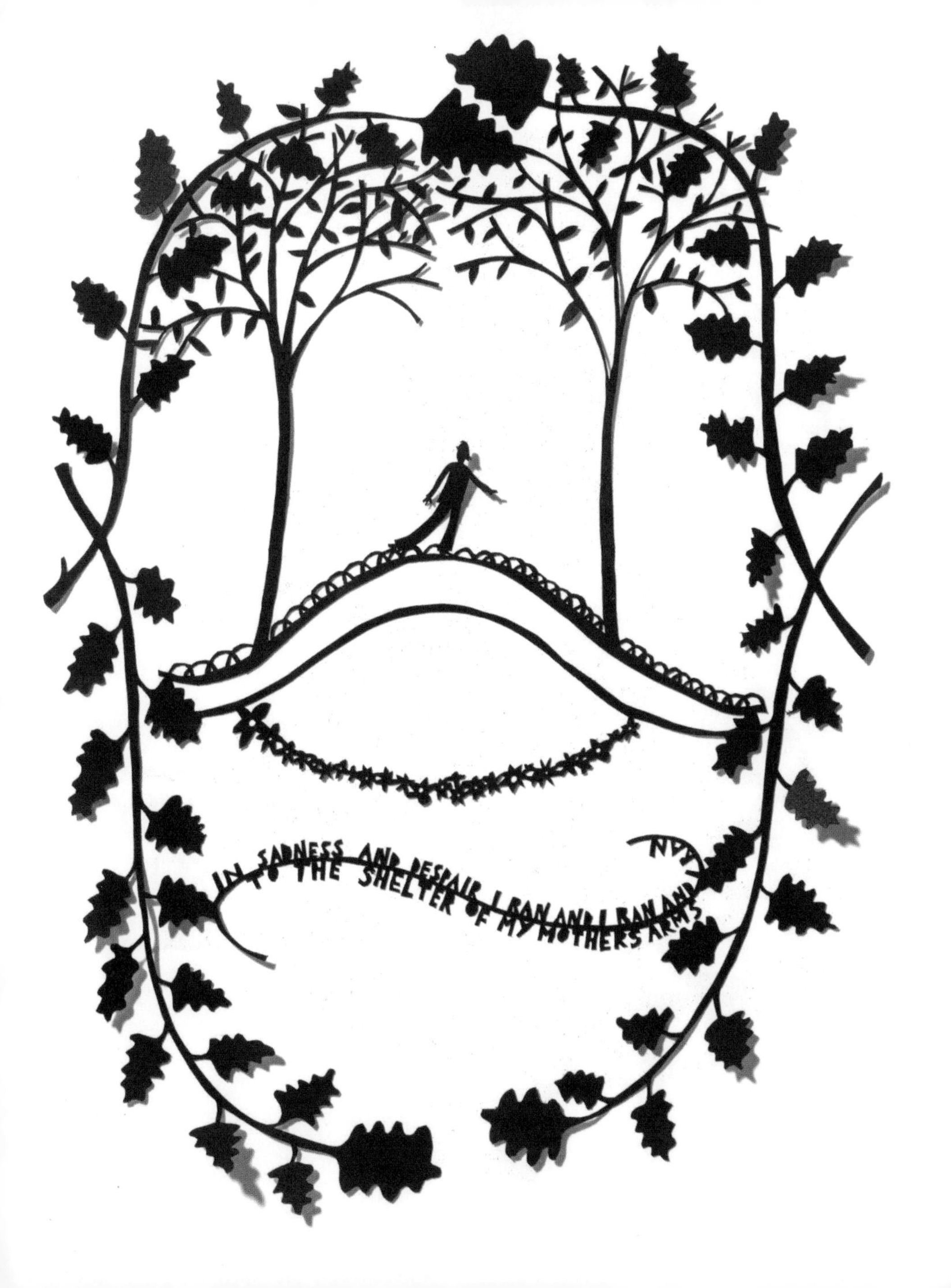
IN SADNESS AND DESPAIR I RAN AND I RAN AND I RAN
TO THE SHELTER OF MY MOTHERS ARMS

Mother of mine
O MOTHER OF MINE
HELP ME PLEASE
TELL ME WHY I FEEL THIS WAY.

I PRESSED MY FACE INTO HER
STILL WARM APRON AND THE OLD SMELLS
IT HELD BEGAN TO MAKE ME FEEL
BETTER INSIDE.

Oh my
Darling.
BLOOD OF
MY BLOOD.
YOU KNOW THAT
MY HEART BEATS IN
TIME WITH YOURS.
WHEN I WAS YOUR AGE
I FELT EXACTLY THE
SAME WAY

The problem is your heart
Is too big for you alone
And with only you inside
It feels like an
empty place

IT NEEDS SOMEONE
IN THERE WITH YOU TO HELP
FILL IT
UP
THIS
IS
WHY
YOUR
WHOLE
LIFE
FEELS
AS IF
SOME
LARGE
NAMELESS
PART
IS
MISSING

I Asked & I begged
Oh Mother of myne
Could YOU
come and live in
here with me?

My Sweet
My Love
If I could I would
But I left my heart
and now I live in your
fathers heart

BUT DO NOT
DESPAIR
BECAUSE
SOMEWHERE
THERE IS A
HEART

THAT IS BEAT-
ING THAT
IS MEANT
JUST FOR
YOU

AND ONE
WILL BE THE
HEART TH-
BEAT INSIDE
AND ON THAT
WILL
WHOLE
FIRST

DAY THIS
OTHER
AT WILL
OF YOU.

DAY YOU
FEEL
FOR THE
TIME.

THIS HEART
WILL BE GROWING AND
YEARNING AS YOUR
HEART GROWS AND
YEARNS

SOMEWHERE
SOMEBODY CLOSER THAN YOU MIGHT THINK

Maybe in this
very city or in
a field a thousand
miles away
BUT YOU MUST
BE PATIENT
AND NEVER DESPAIR
FOR ONE DAY YOU SHALL SURELY FIND EACHOTHER

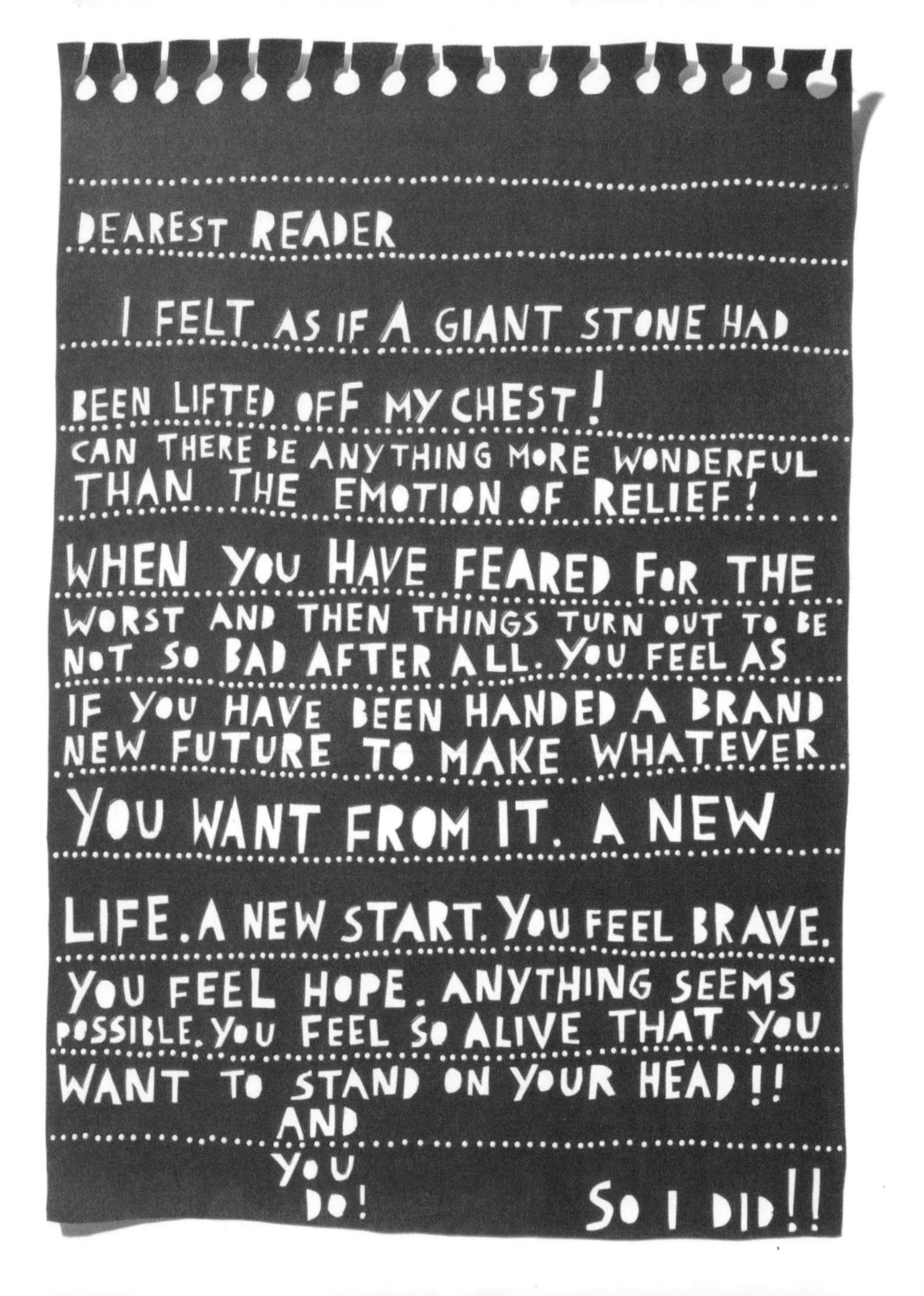
DEAREST READER
I FELT AS IF A GIANT STONE HAD
BEEN LIFTED OFF MY CHEST!
CAN THERE BE ANYTHING MORE WONDERFUL
THAN THE EMOTION OF RELIEF!
WHEN YOU HAVE FEARED FOR THE
WORST AND THEN THINGS TURN OUT TO BE
NOT SO BAD AFTER ALL. YOU FEEL AS
IF YOU HAVE BEEN HANDED A BRAND
NEW FUTURE TO MAKE WHATEVER
YOU WANT FROM IT. A NEW
LIFE. A NEW START. YOU FEEL BRAVE.
YOU FEEL HOPE. ANYTHING SEEMS
POSSIBLE. YOU FEEL SO ALIVE THAT YOU
WANT TO STAND ON YOUR HEAD!!
AND
YOU
DO!
SO I DID!!

THAT NIGHT IN MY SMALL BED IN MY SMALL ROOM I FELT STRANGELY AT PEACE.
SANDWICHED BETWEEN THE STARS AND THE EARTH I FELT SMALL AND INSIGNIFICANT. I REMEMBERED ONCE LOOKING THROUGH THE WINDOW OF A PLANE AND THINKING HOW GIANT MOUNTAINS SEEMED ONLY AS HIGH AS THE RIDGES OF YOUR FINGERPRINTS AND THE DEEPEST CANYONS HARDLY EVEN SEEMED TO SCRATCH THE SURFACE. IT MADE YOU THINK 'WHAT IS ALL THE FUSS ABOUT?'
AND I LET THE COMFORT OF MY OWN SMALLNESS HOLD ME AS I FELL ASLEEP.

THE FOLLOWING
MORNING I CLIMBED UP TO MY WINDOW
TO WISH THE DAY A WARM HELLO.

WHEN YOU ARE A CHILD THE
FUTURE ALWAYS SEEMS SO
FAR AWAY. BUT NOW IT
SEEMED TO HAVE TAKEN A GIANT
LEAP NEARER. WHAT DOES A CHILD
KNOW OF LOVE ? I DONT KNOW. I
HAD ONLY JUST TURNED TWELVE

BUT STILL I AS AN OLD MAN WRITING
THESE REMINISCENCES SO MANY YEARS
LATER I CAN HONESTLY SAY I
FELT NO DIFFERENT AT THAT
AGE THAN I DO TODAY. THAT
IS TO SAY AS FULL OF LONGING
AS I EVER WAS.

YOU KNOW
YOU WANT TO SAY
SOMETHING BUT WHAT?
YOU KNOW YOU HAVE TO SAY
SOMETHING BUT HOW
BUT NOTHING HAPPENS UNTIL
YOU SAY THE FIRST WORD OR WRITE
THE FIRST LETTER OR CUT THE
FIRST LINE. AND SO I STARTED....

I AM NOT ALONE
I AM NOT ALONE
I AM NOT ALONE
And I Wrote And I wrote
YOU ARE NOT ALONE
YOU ARE NOT ALONE
YOU ARE NOT ALONE
And I wrote And I wrote And I wrote
THIS IS FOR YOU
THIS IS FOR YOU
THIS IS FOR YOU

AND IT FELT BETTER
WHY DOES PUTTING THINGS DOWN ON PAPER SOMEHOW MAKE THINGS SEEM MORE MANAGEABLE?
IS IT BECAUSE IT IS A CONSTRUCTIVE ACT WHEN INSIDE YOU FEEL DESTROYED?

EVEN THOUGH
YOU MAY FEEL EMPTY INSIDE CAN IT MAKE
YOU FEEL BETTER BY WRITING WORDS?
WHAT KIND OF MAGIC IS THIS? AND YOU
LOOK UP AT THE STARS AND WONDER IS
THIS HOW GOD FELT WHEN HE CREATED
THE UNIVERSE

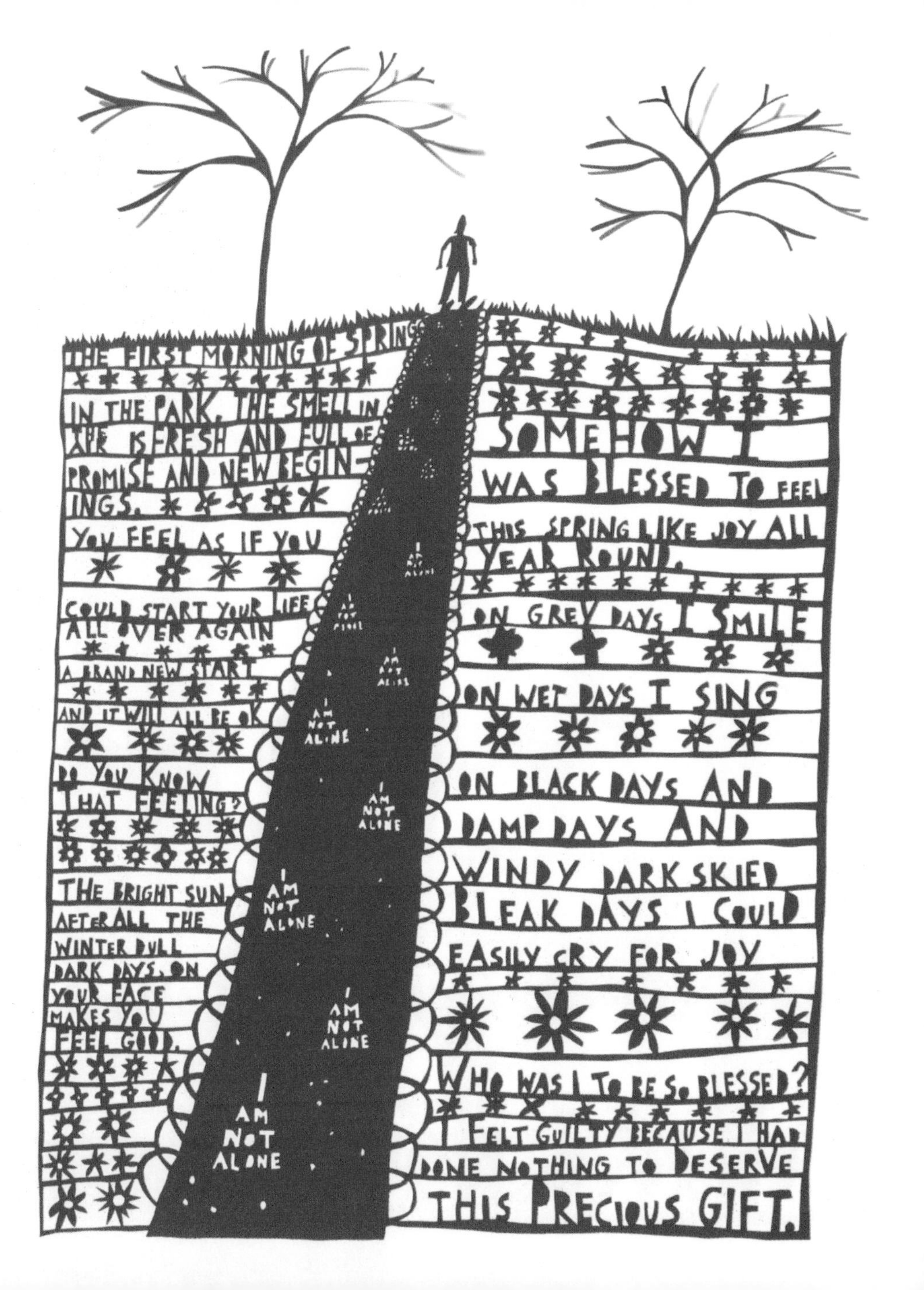
THE FIRST MORNING OF SPRING
IN THE PARK, THE SMELL IN
THE AIR IS FRESH AND FULL OF
PROMISE AND NEW BEGIN-
INGS.
YOU FEEL AS IF YOU
COULD START YOUR LIFE
ALL OVER AGAIN
A BRAND NEW START
AND IT WILL ALL BE OK
DO YOU KNOW
THAT FEELING?
THE BRIGHT SUN
AFTER ALL THE
WINTER DULL
DARK DAYS, ON
YOUR FACE
MAKES YOU
FEEL GOOD.
I AM NOT ALONE
I AM NOT ALONE
I AM NOT ALONE
I AM NOT ALONE
I AM NOT ALONE
SOMEHOW I
WAS BLESSED TO FEEL
THIS SPRING LIKE JOY ALL
YEAR ROUND.
ON GREY DAYS I SMILE
ON WET DAYS I SING
ON BLACK DAYS AND
DAMP DAYS AND
WINDY DARK SKIED
BLEAK DAYS I COULD
EASILY CRY FOR JOY
WHO WAS I TO BE SO BLESSED?
I FELT GUILTY BECAUSE I HAD
DONE NOTHING TO DESERVE
THIS PRECIOUS GIFT.

I DISCOVERED THAT IN A BUSY PLACE IF YOU
MAKE YOURSELF LOOK BUSY YOU CAN BECOME
INVISIBLE. I FOUND MYSELF A BIG LADDER AND
PROCEEDED TO DISAPPEAR

THIS IS ME NOW
(LOOK! CAN YOU SEE)
SO YOUNG AND SO PRECIOUS
WHAT WILL I BE?
(LOOK INTO THE FUTURE)
HOW WILL I SEEM THEN
(HOLD UP A MIRROR AND
STILL THE SAME FACE
LOOKS BACK)
BUT REALLY NOT SO
DIFFERENT
ONLY OLDER BUT STILL
ME

TO
MAKE
ME FEEL
ALIVE
WITH
LIFE
AND
LOVE
TOES
AND AROUN
MY ANKLES.
THIS WATER IS
DEEP
ENOUGH

NO STEPPING STONES FOR ME BECAUSE I CHOOSE TO
SIT ON MY LADDER AND FEEL THE ICY WATER FLOW BETWEEN MY

WHAT WAS IMPORTANT
I DONT KNOW ANYMORE.

WHAT HAPPENS WHEN YOU
SEE LESS AND LESS THE
GOOD AND MORE AND
MORE THE BAD?
IS THAT WHEN YOU
BEGIN TO DIE?

I HAVE THIS FEELING
OF LONGING FOR
SOMETHING THAT
WILL LAST.

THAT WILL
IMPROVE.

THE THOUGHT OF
IMPROVEMENT
GIVES ME HOPE.
WITHOUT HOPE I WONT SURVIVE
I
JUST WANT
THINGS TO
IMPROVE.

I PROMISE THAT ONE DAY I WILL TAKE
YOU TO THE QUIETEST PLACES
WHERE ALL YOU CAN HEAR IS
THE WHISTLING OF THE WIND THROUGH THE AIR

DONT JUST LOOK
AT AND ENJOY THE
BEAUTY
OF A GLORIOUS VIEW
LOOK
AT
EVERYTHING
AND SEE THE
GOODNESS OF IT
BECAUSE ITS ALL OUT THERE WAITING FOR YOU
STRAIGHT HAIR AND AFRO HAIR
SMALL BOYS AND OLD WOMEN
GOLDFISH AND WHALES
SPARROWS AND EMUS
DESERTS AND GLACIERS
ELEPHANTS AND LITTLE ANTS

I PROMISE THAT ONE DAY I
WILL TAKE YOU TO THE
LOUDEST PLACES

I PROMISE THAT ONE
DAY I WILL TAKE YOU TO
THE HIGHEST PLACES

THIS BELL WILL RING WHEN YOU THINK OF WHO I MIGHT BE
THIS BELL WILL RING WHEN I DREAM A DREAM OF GOOD
THIS BELL WILL RING WHEN I AM ALONE
THIS BELL WILL RING WHEN I THINK OF WHO YOU MIGHT BE

THIS
BELL WILL
THIS
BELL WILL
RING WHEN
I FEEL
NO HOPE
THIS
BELL WILL
RING WHEN I
HOLD YOU
IN MY
ARMS
THIS
BELL WILL
RING
WHEN FROM
NOTHING
SOMETHING
COMES.

AND
SO
I PAINTED
AND I DREW
AND I CUT OUT
PAPER AND ALL
OVER TOWN I
LEFT MY
MESSAGES
FOR YOU
TO ONE
DAY
FIND

MY HOME
WILL HAVE
NO WINDOWS
DOORS OR FLOORS
NOR BRICKS OR MORTAR
I CARE NAUGHT FOR THEM.
MY ONLY HOME
IS IN YOUR ARMS
And nowhere else
EXCEPT PERHAPS
IN THESE MANY TINY
SCRAPS OF DREAMS
AND PAPER

IF I WAS THIRSTy WOULD I DRAW A DRINK?
IF I WASHOMELESS WOULD I DRAW A HOUSE?
IF I WAS LONELY WOULD I DRAW A PICTURE OF YOU?
IF I WAS HUNGRY WOULD I DRAW FOOD?

BUT WHAT IF I HAD EVERYTHING THAT
I COULD EVER WANT?
WHAT WOULD BE LEFT TO DRAW
WHAT LEFT TO SAY?
I DON'T KNOW IF
I COULD BEAR THAT

AND DAY BY
DAY I FILLED
MY WORLD
WITH MORE
WORDS
AND
MORE
DREAMS
AND
MY HEART
BECAME
A PLACE
WHERE I
COULD
ESCAPE
TO
AND
TALK
TO YOU
(WHO
EVER
YOU
MIGHT
TURN
OUT TO BE)
AND HOLD
YOU CLOSE.

AND YEARS FROM NOW
I WILL RETURN AND
SEE THAT WIND AND RAIN
HAVE WASHED THESE WORDS
AWAY, BUT THEY STAYED IN
MY HEART TO THIS DAY
AND I PUT THEM IN THIS
BOOK THAT IS FOR YOU.

ALL OF THESE
THOUGHTS WERE OF YOU
ALL OF THESE
DREAMS WERE OF YOU.
AND MY DARLING
THAT LONELY BOY
STILL LIVES INSIDE ME.
I HAVE NOT CHANGED.
THOSE PROMISES I MADE TO YOU
I WILL FULFIL.

for DAVID

First published in Great Britain in 2007 by Hodder & Stoughton
A division of Hodder Headline

A Sceptre book

1

A CIP catalogue record for this title is available from the British Library

ISBN 978 0 340 93367 1

Photography by Packshot Factory
Printed and bound in Italy by Graphicom Srl

Hodder Headline's policy is to use papers that are natural, renewable and recyclable products and made from wood grown in sustainable forests. The logging and manufacturing processes are expected to conform to the environmental regulations of the country of origin.

Hodder & Stoughton Ltd
A division of Hodder Headline
338 Euston Road
London NW1 3BH

Thanks to Hazel and Louise.